...AND A NAP!

THIS TEACHER NEEDS A MOTHER FUCKING BEER

A SWEAR WORD COLORING BOOK FOR ADULTS

Want free goodies?
Email us at freebies@honeybadgercoloring.com

@honeybadgercoloring

Honey Badger Coloring

Shop our other books at
www.honeybadgercoloring.com

Wholesale distribution through Ingram Content Group
www.ingramcontent.com/publishers/distribution/wholesale

For questions and customer service, email us at
support@honeybadgercoloring.com

TEACHER.
EDUCATOR.
MENTOR.
FUCKING.
LEGEND.

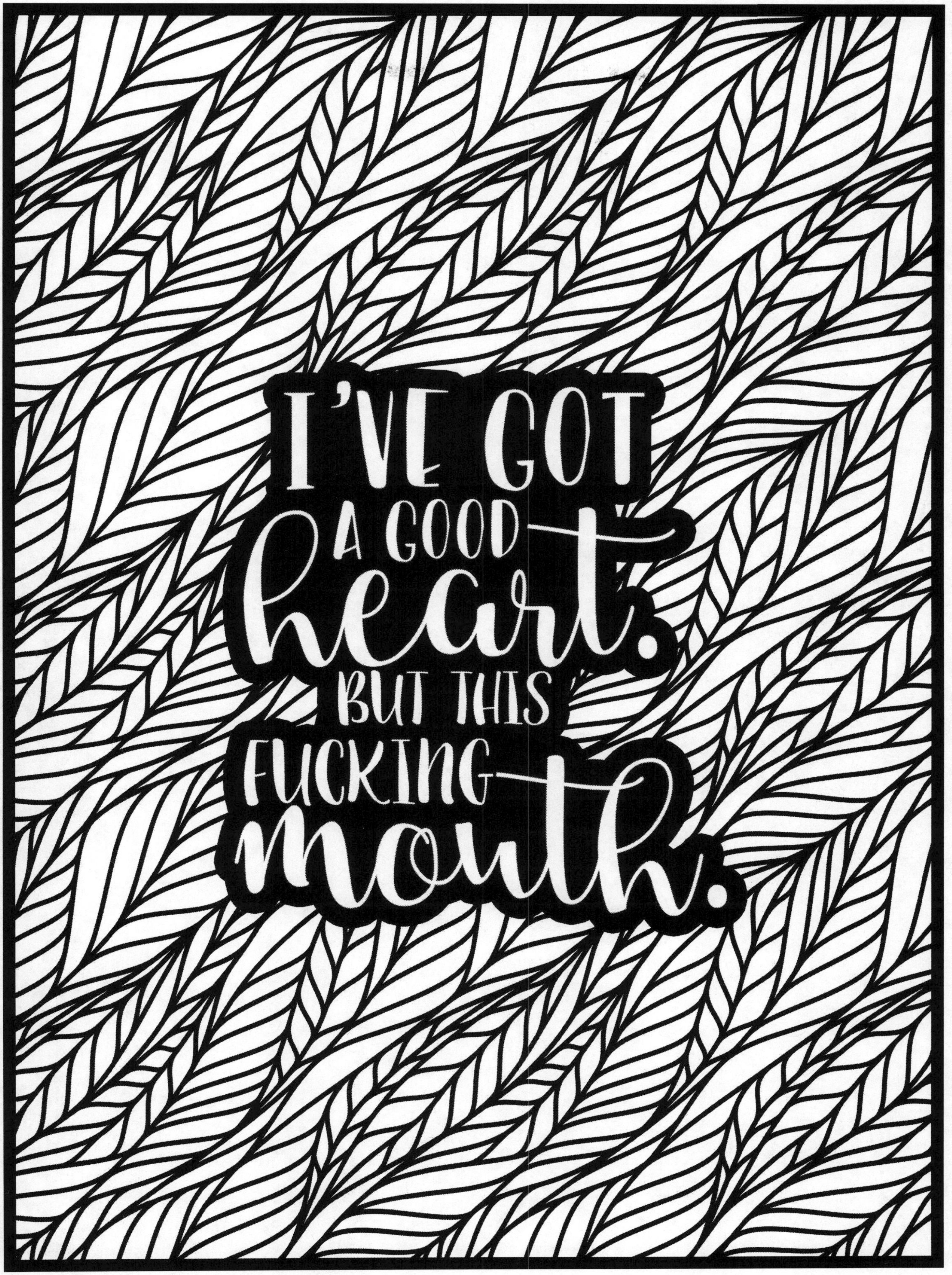
I'VE GOT
A GOOD
heart.
BUT THIS
FUCKING
mouth.

Bad
Bitch

Cheer up
and
chuck it
in
the
fuckit
bucket

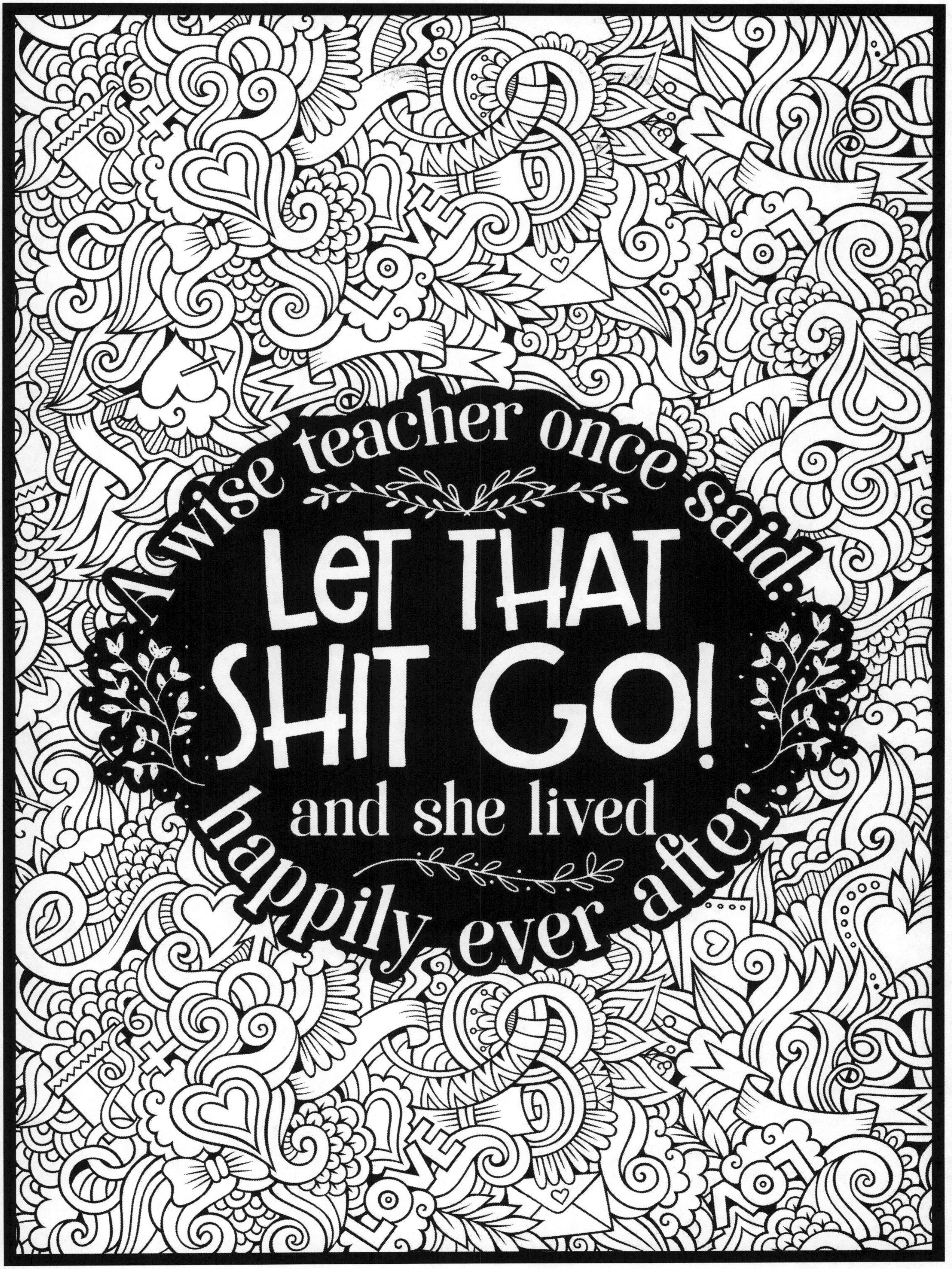
A wise teacher once said...
LET THAT
SHIT GO!
and she lived
happily ever after...

I SUFFER FROM
RESTING
TEACHER
FACE

I ♥
MY
fucking
STUDENTS.

I'm
a fucking
UNICORN
B·I·T·C·H

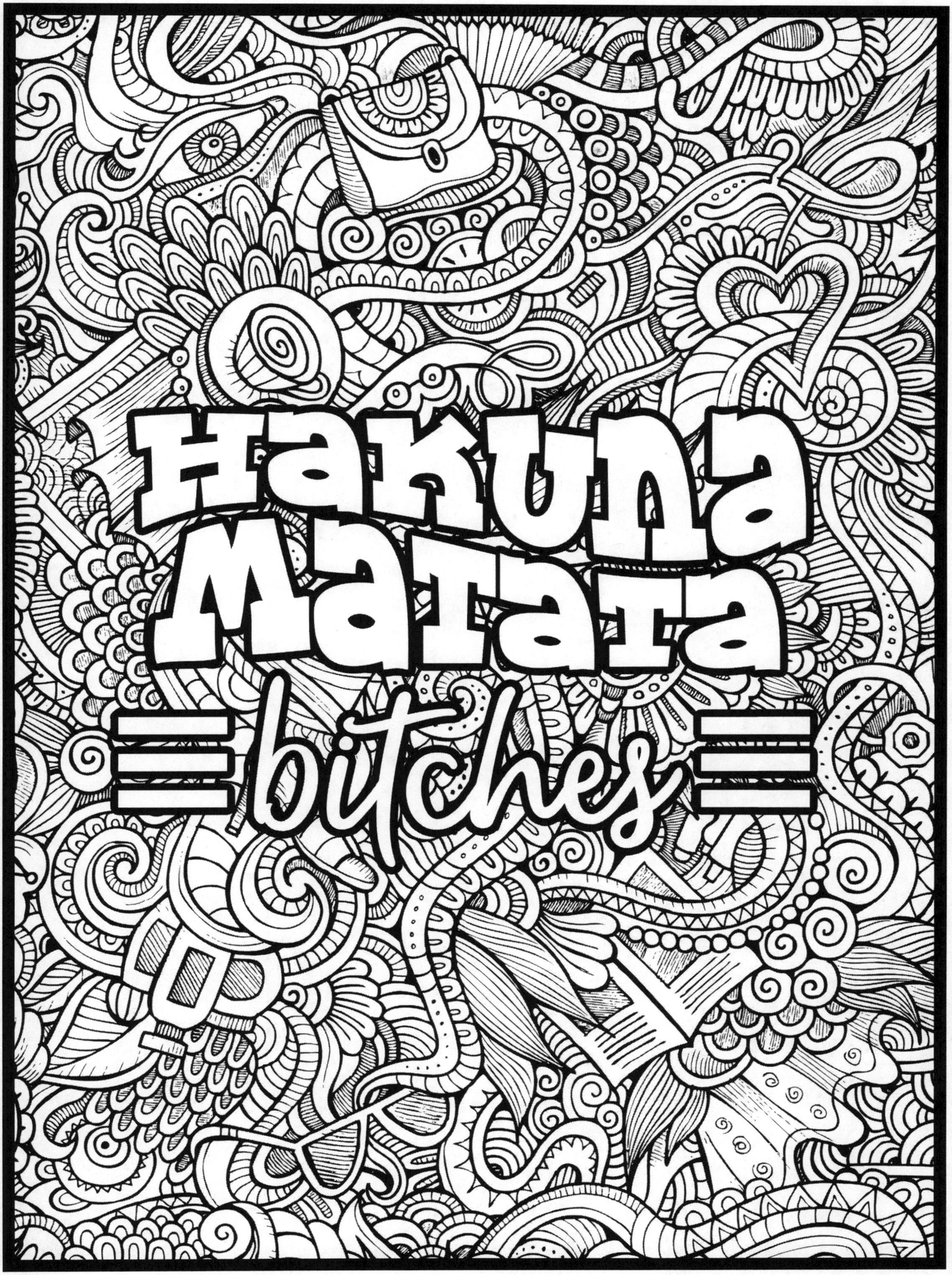
Hakuna
Matata
bitches

ALLERGIC
to
BULLSHIT

BAD
ASS
TEACHER

I'm
a delicate
FUCKIN'
FLOWER

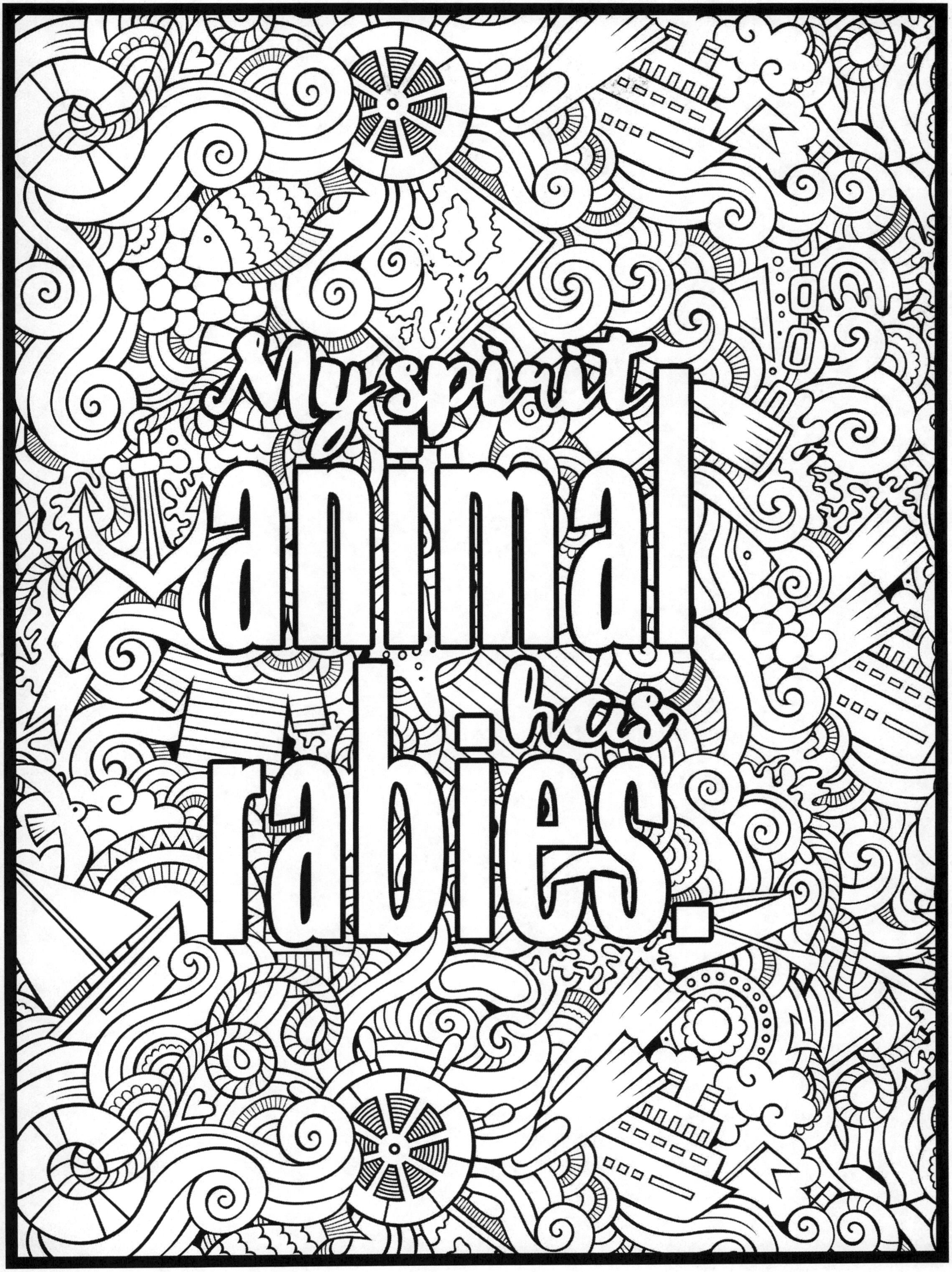
My spirit
animal
has
rabies.

CLASSY
BITCH

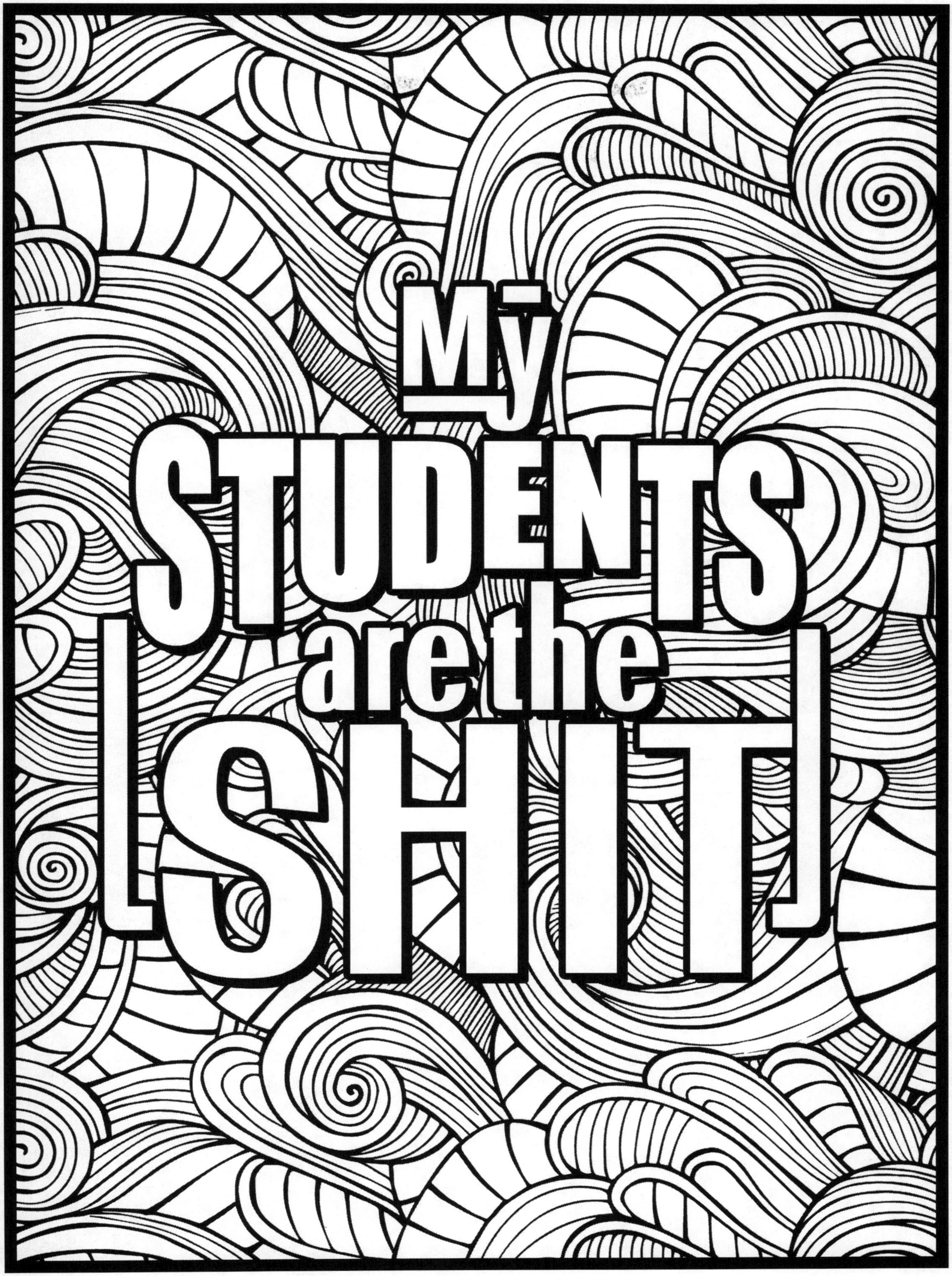
My
STUDENTS
are the
SHIT

KINDNESS.
Sprinkle
THAT
SHIT
EVERYWHERE!

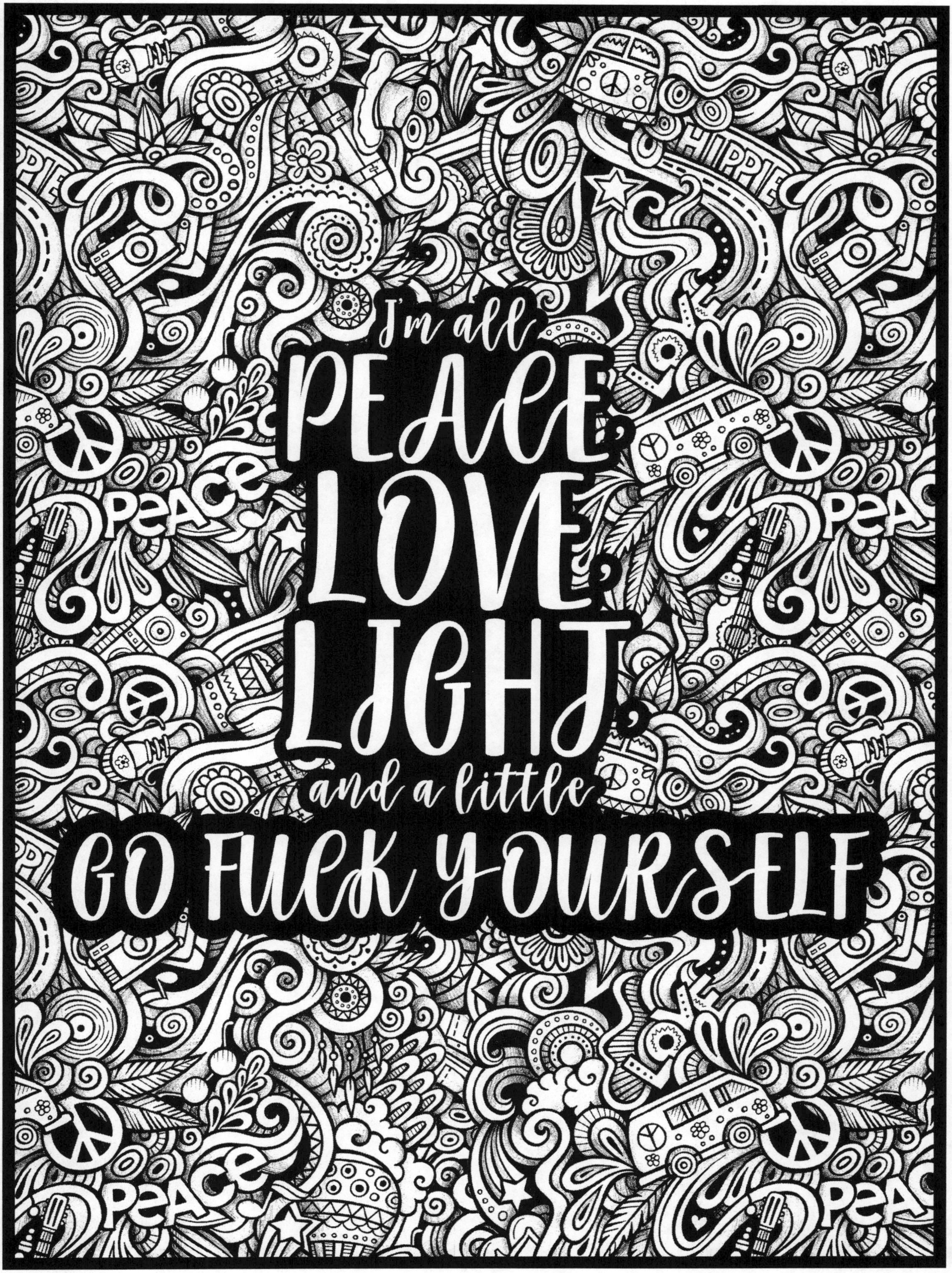
I'm all
PEACE,
LOVE,
LIGHT,
and a little
GO FUCK YOURSELF
HIPPIE
PEACE

IT IS
WHAT IT
FUCKING
IS

Fresh
OUT OF
fucks

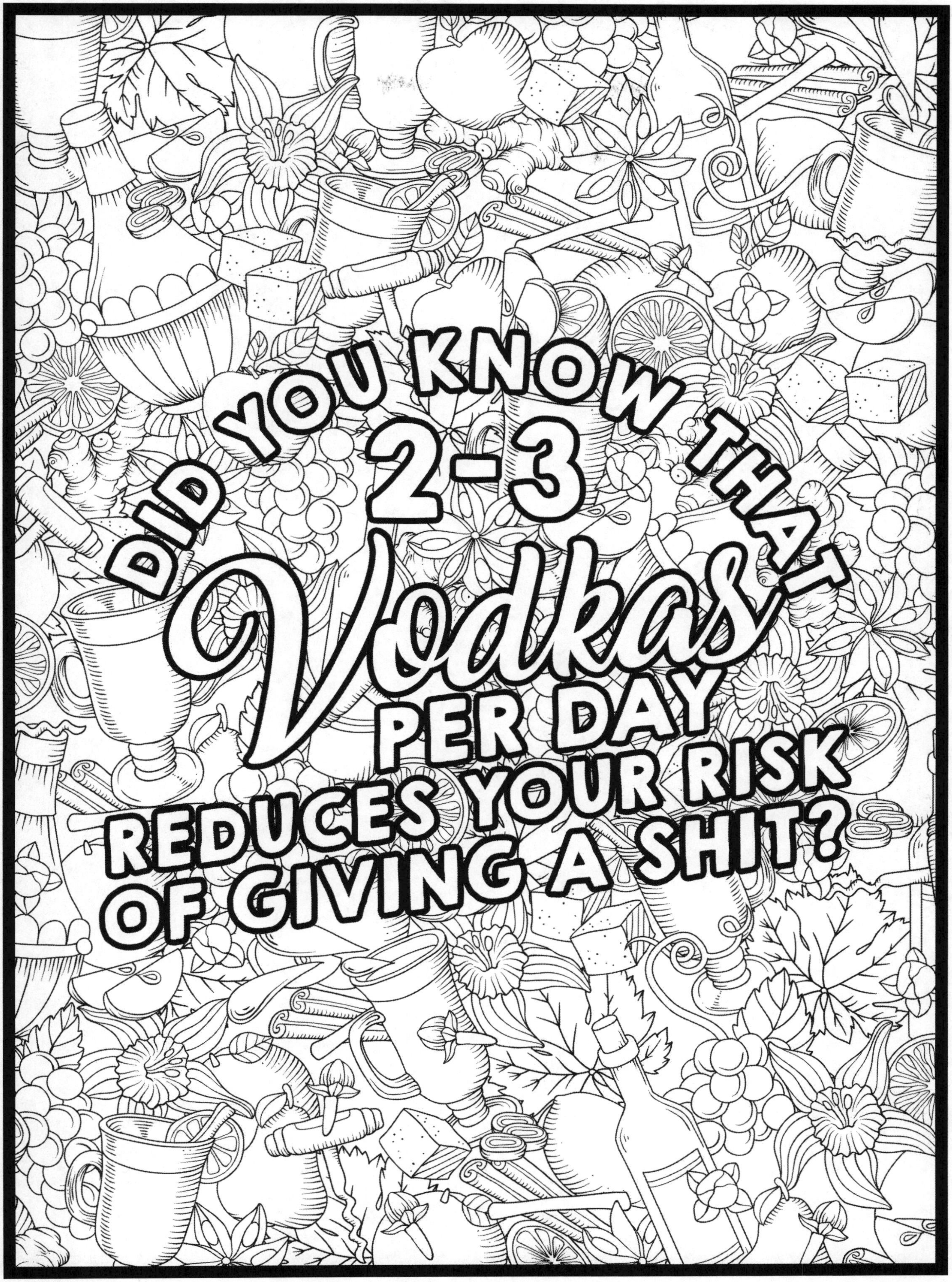
DID YOU KNOW THAT
2-3
Vodkas
PER DAY
REDUCES YOUR RISK
OF GIVING A SHIT?

Let me check my
GIVEASHITOMETER.
NOPE,
nothing.

SHIT
happens

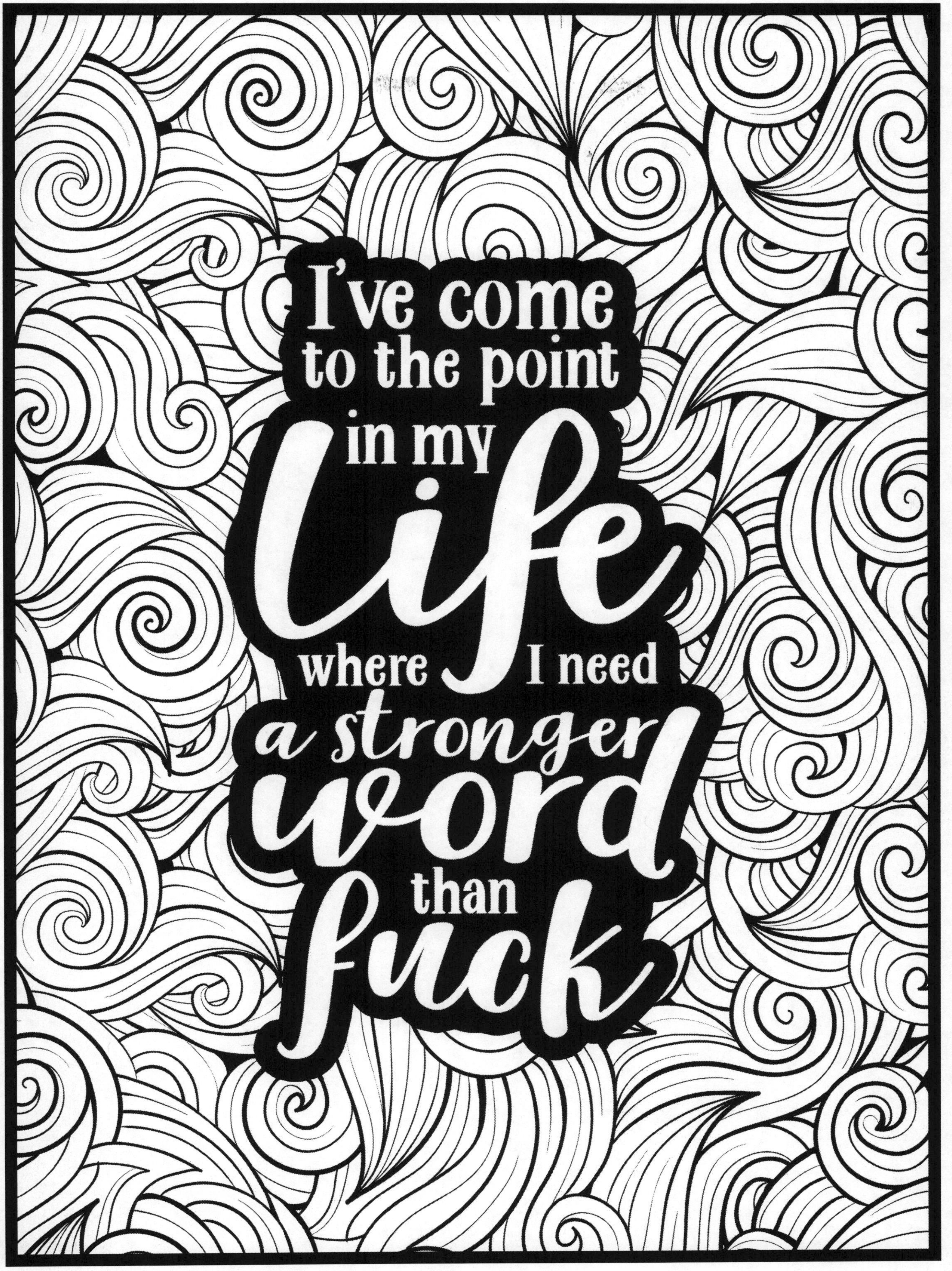
I've come
to the point
in my
life
where I need
a stronger
word
than
fuck

AND ON THAT DAY
not a
Single
Fuck
WAS GIVEN

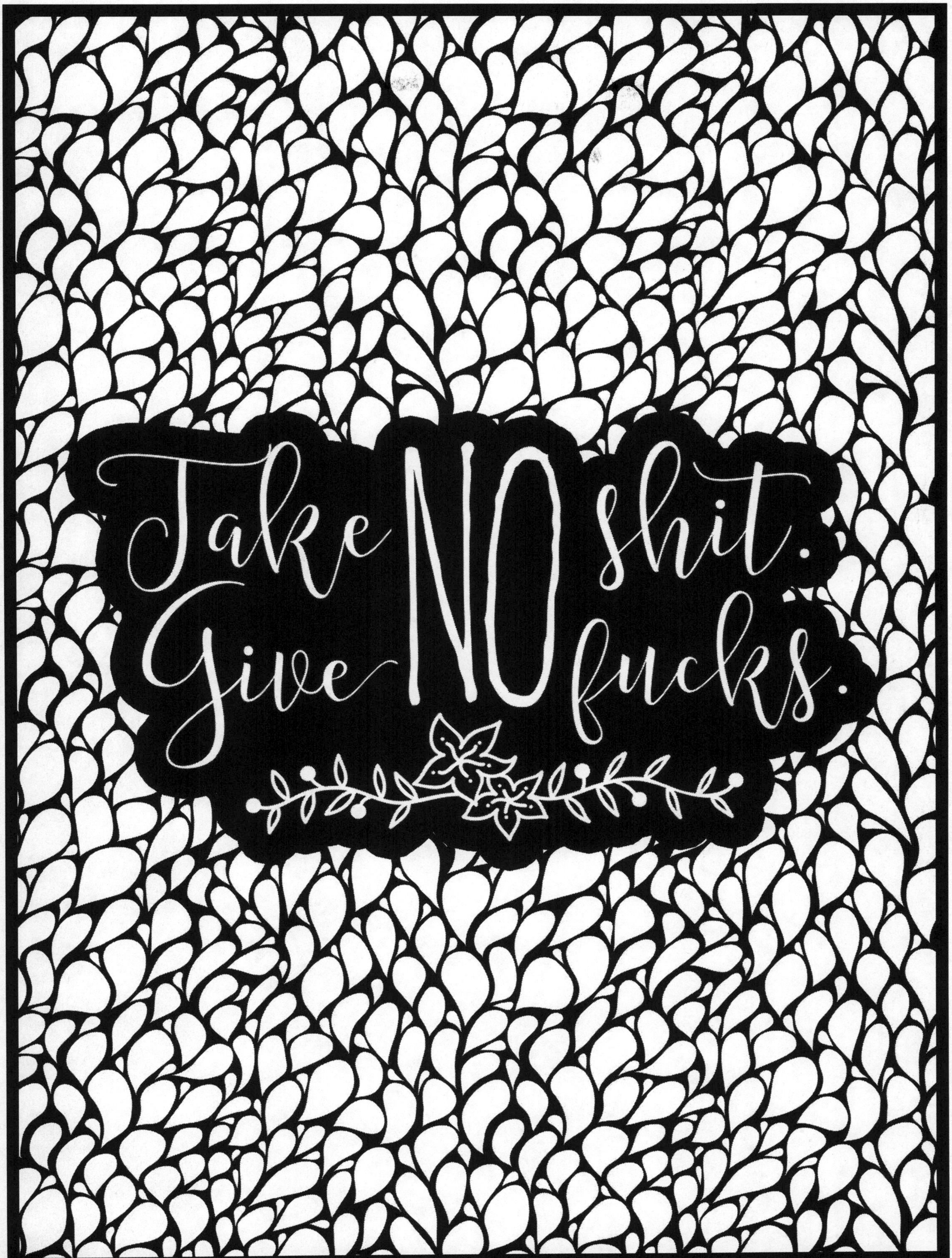
Take NO shit.
Give NO fucks.

I SWEAR
BECAUSE
I CARE

ABSO
fucking
LUTELY

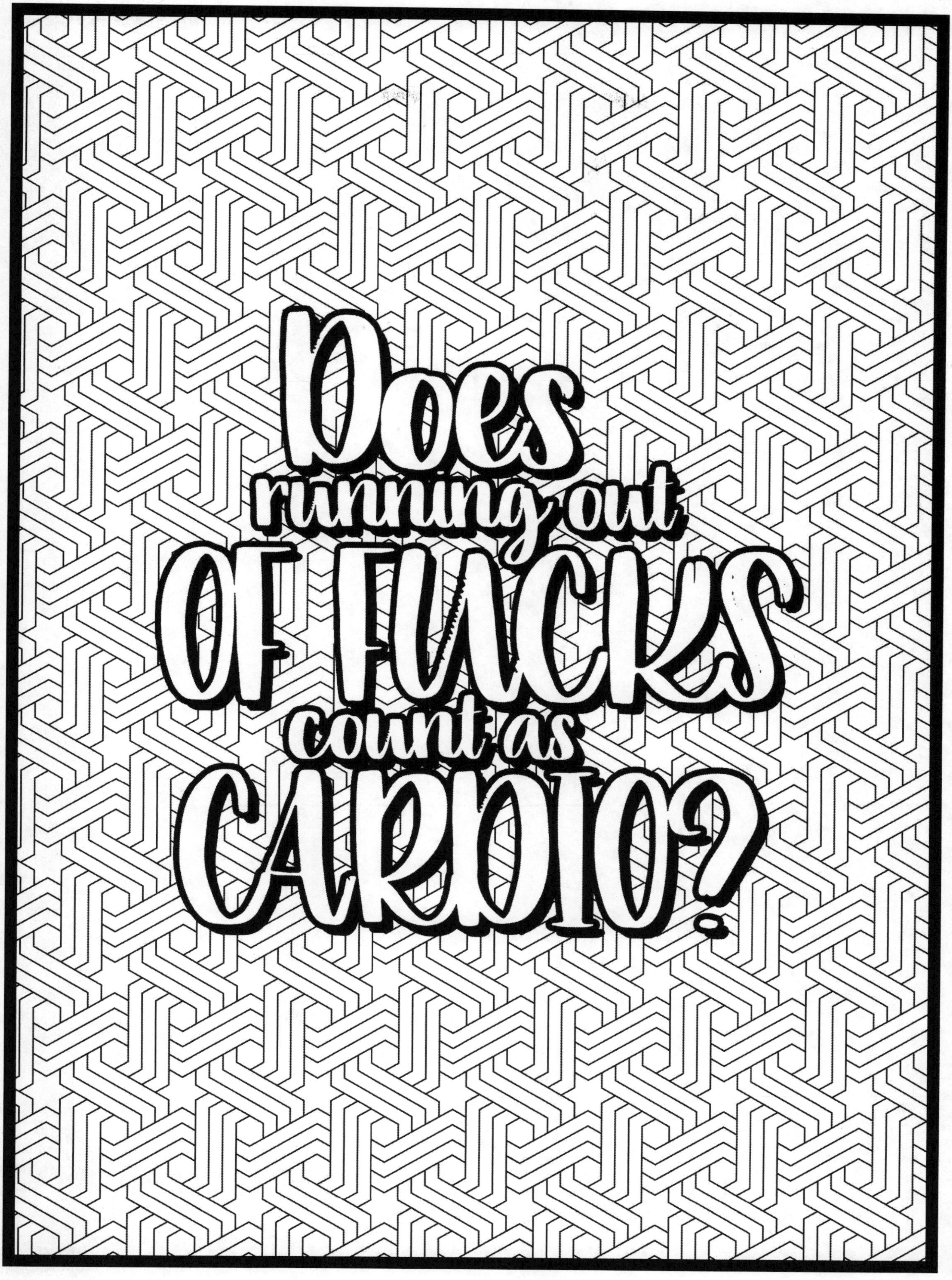
Does
running out
OF FUCKS
count as
CARDIO?

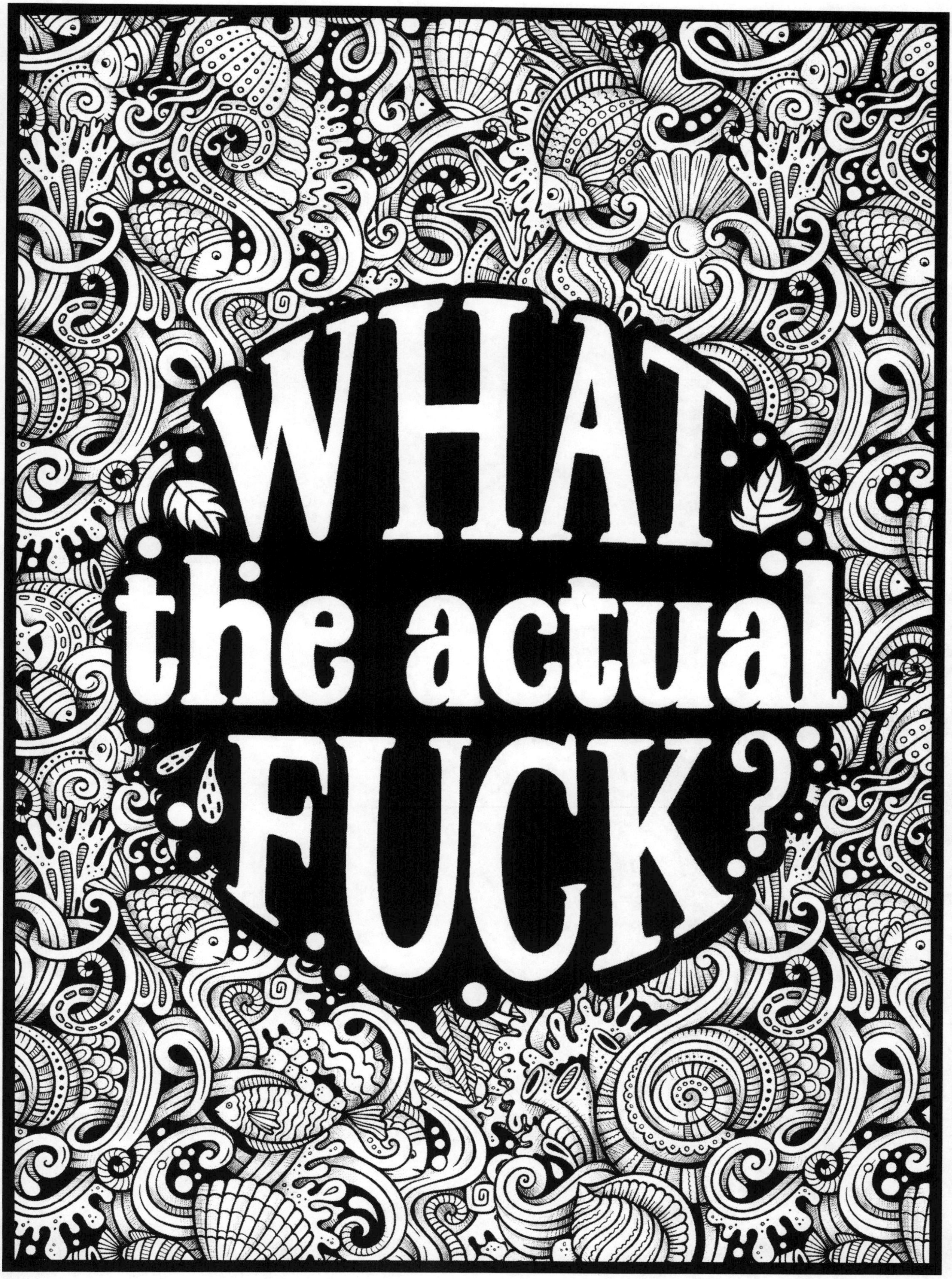
WHAT
the actual
FUCK?

I'm a
happy
go
lucky
ray
of fucking
sunshine

THE SOUND
I like
you make when you
SHUT THE
FUCK UP

Shit IN
ONE HAND.
Wish in
THE
other,
AND SEE
WHICH
fills up first

I RUN ON
caffeine,
SARCASM
&
F-BOMBS

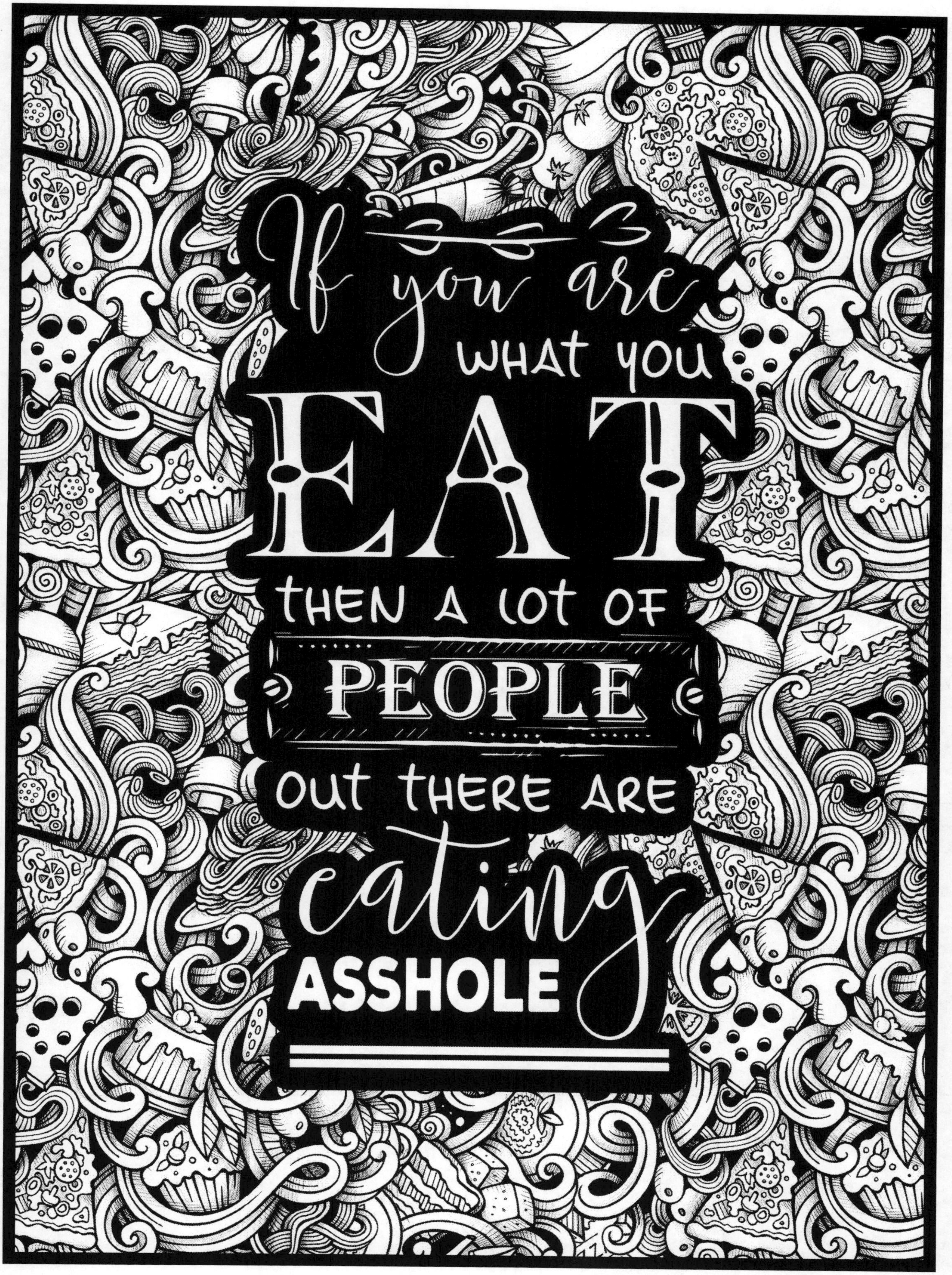
If you are
what you
EAT
then a lot of
PEOPLE
out there are
eating
ASSHOLE

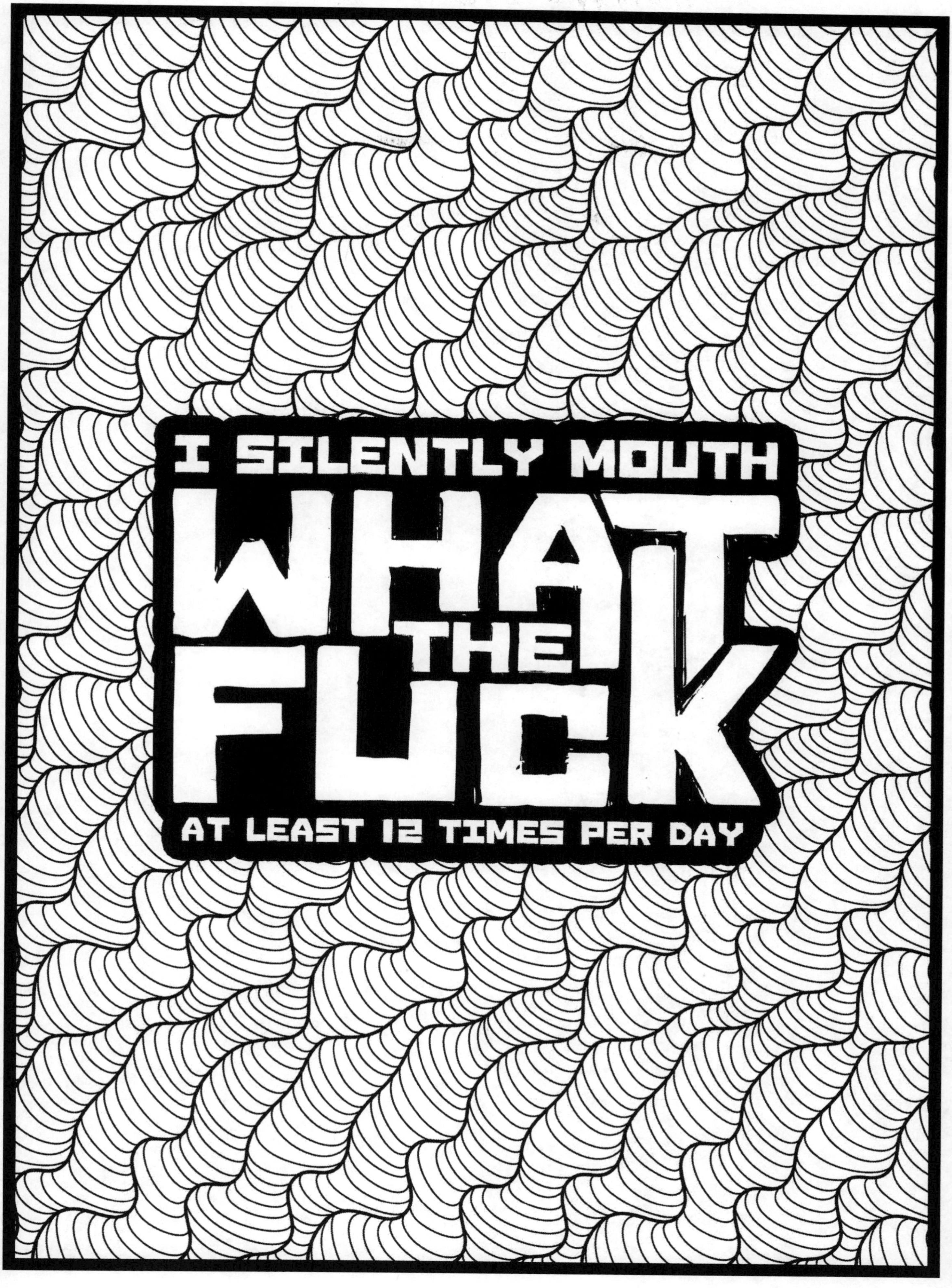
I SILENTLY MOUTH
WHAT
THE
FUCK
AT LEAST 12 TIMES PER DAY

I'VE TRIED
to STOP
SWEARING
BUT
I CUNT

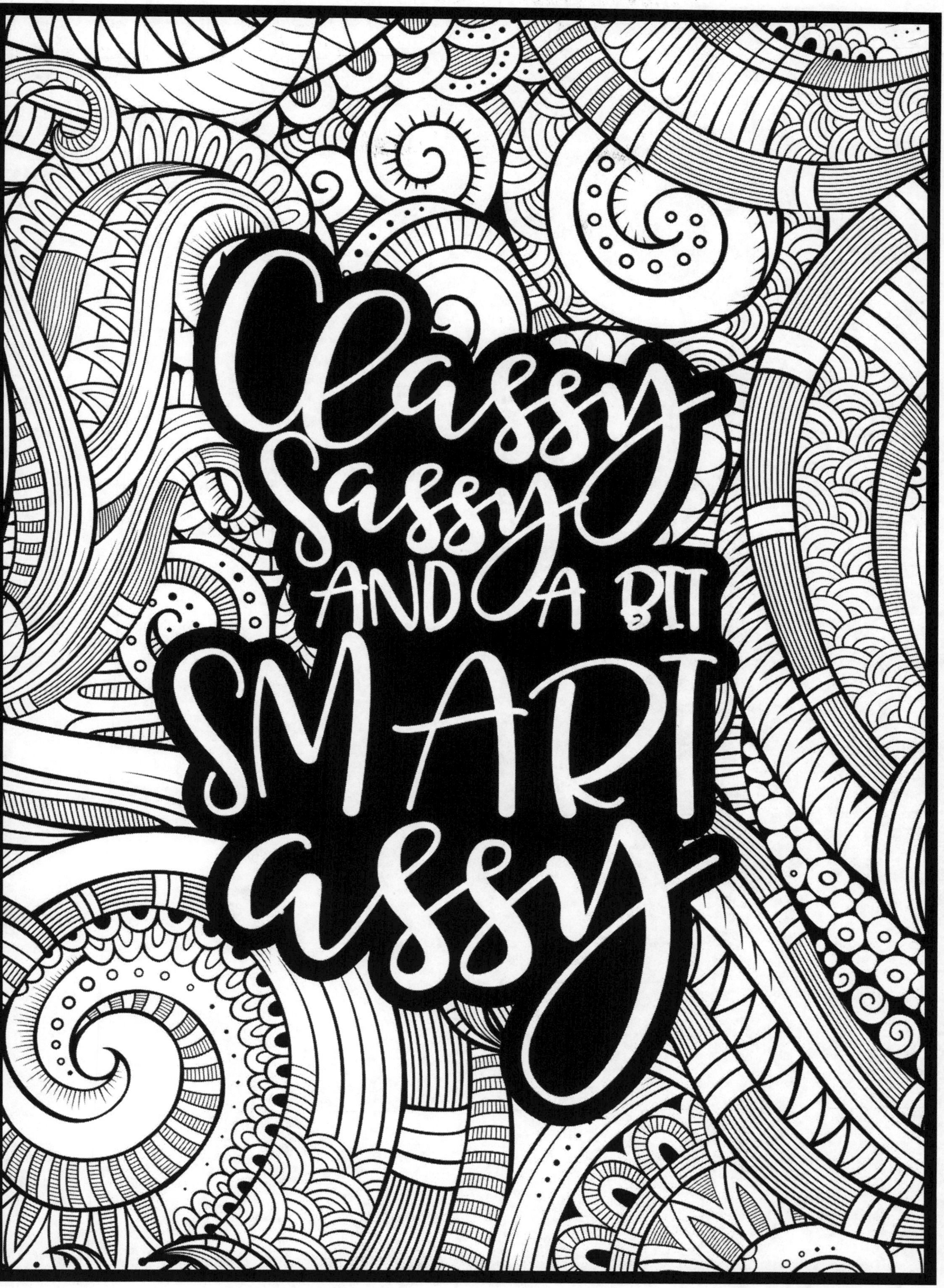
Classy
Sassy
AND A BIT
SMART
assy

WHY DON'T YOU SLIP INTO
SOMETHING MORE
comfy,
LIKE A
Coma

Well
AREN'T WE
JUST A RAY
of FUCKING
Sunshine

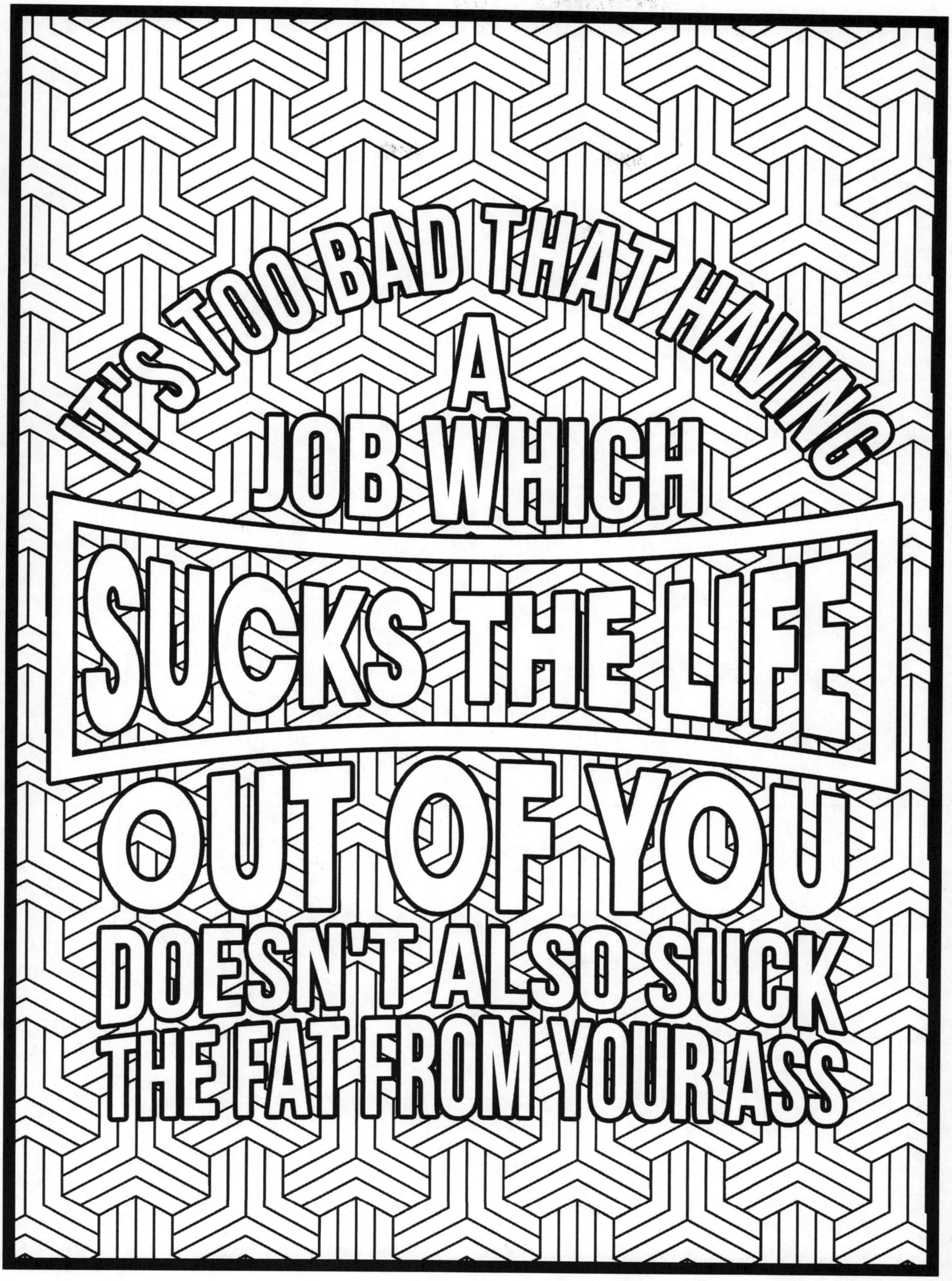
IT'S TOO BAD THAT HAVING
A
JOB WHICH
SUCKS THE LIFE
OUT OF YOU
DOESN'T ALSO SUCK
THE FAT FROM YOUR ASS

Admitting
YOU'RE AN
ASSHOLE
is the
FIRST STEP

Friday
IS MY SECOND
FAVORITE F-WORD

the WORLD
IS NOT FULL
of ASSHOLES but,
THEY ARE STRATEGICALLY
placed
SO THAT YOU'LL COME ACROSS ONE
EVERY
DAY

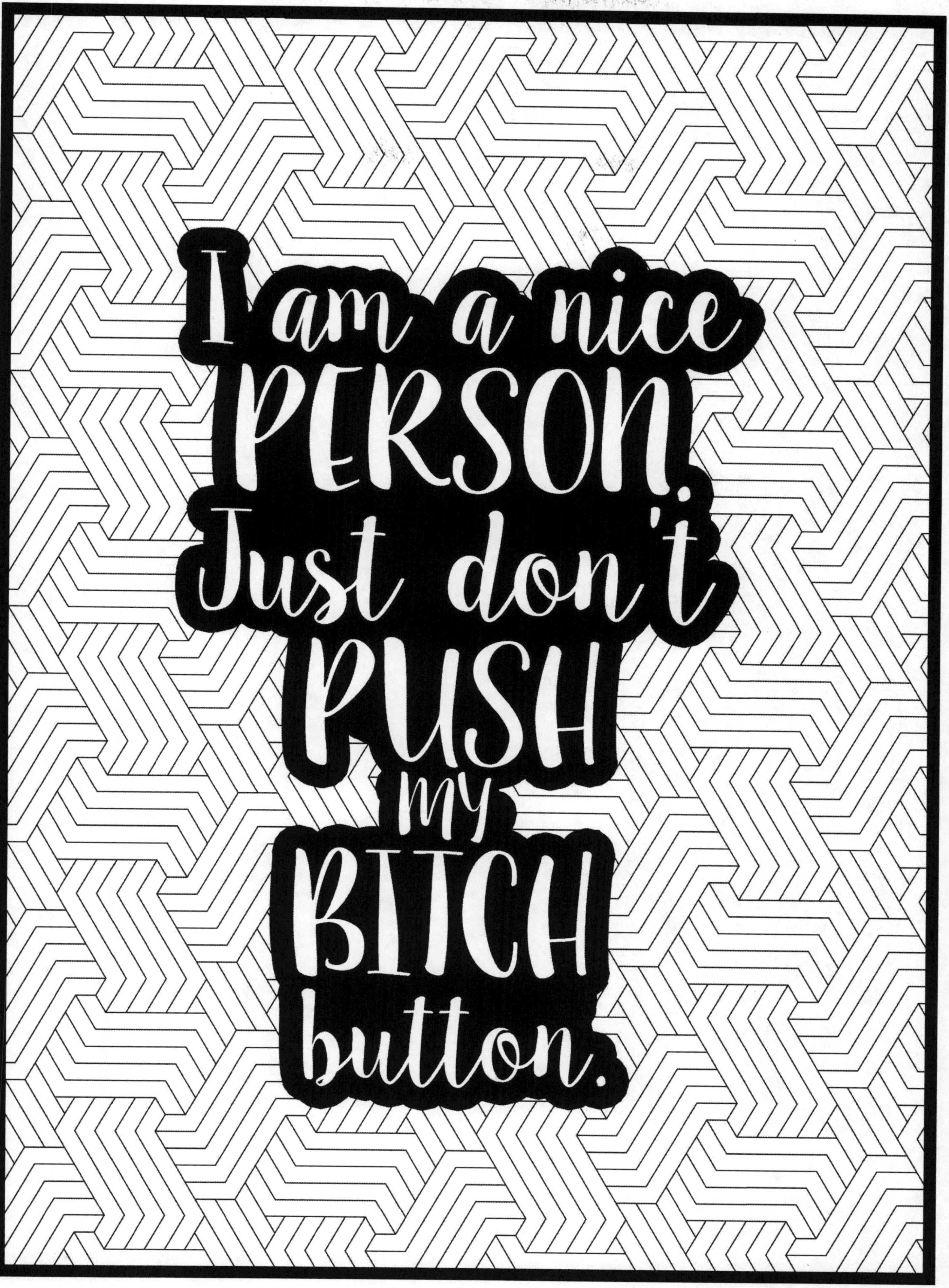
I am a nice
PERSON.
Just don't
PUSH
my
BITCH
button.

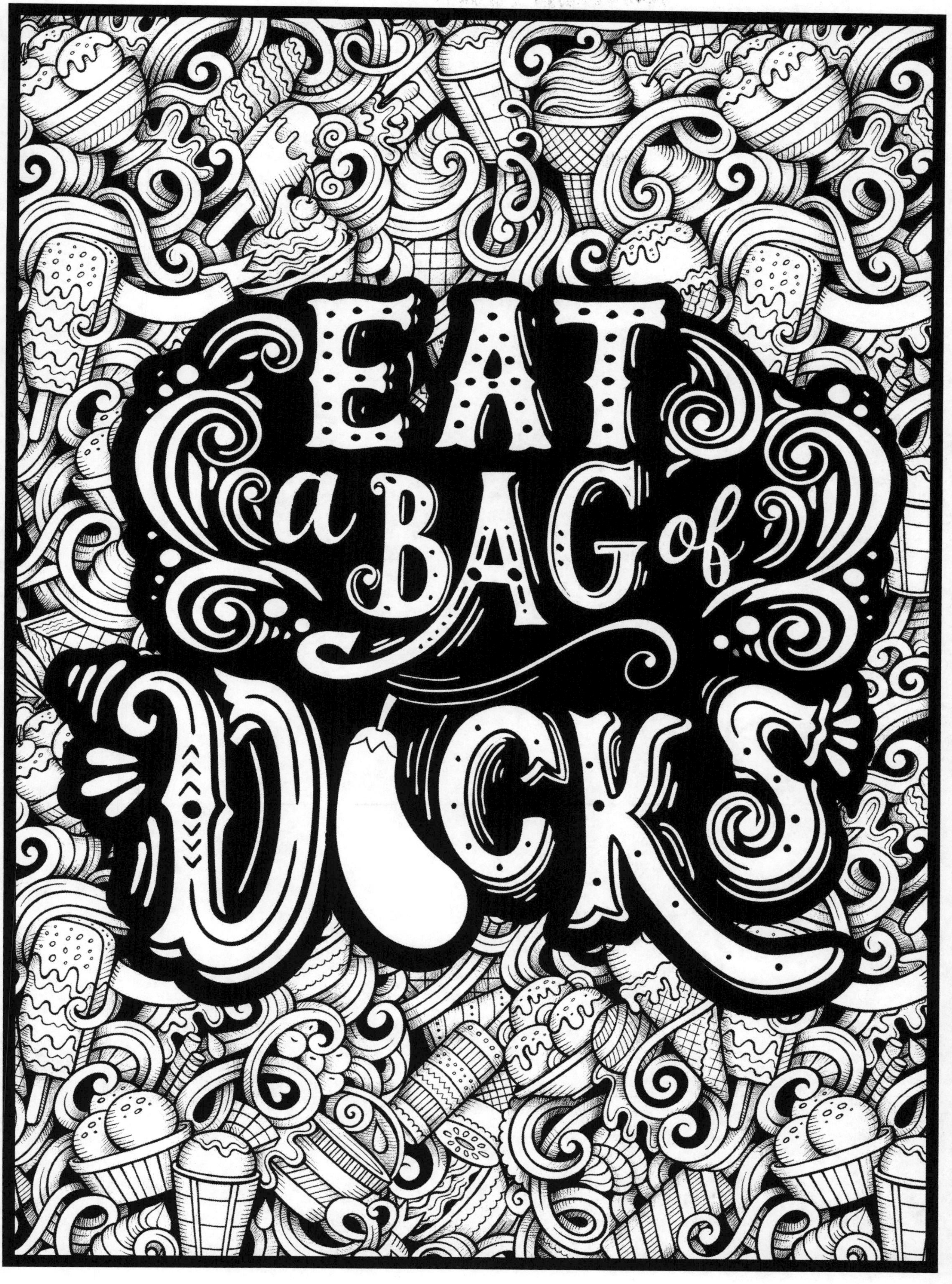
EAT
a BAG of
DICKS

I'm not saying I
hate you,
BUT I WOULD
UNPLUG
your
life
support to
charge my
phone

CALM
THE FUCK
DOWN

LOOKS LIKE IT'S
Fuck
THIS
Shit
O'clock

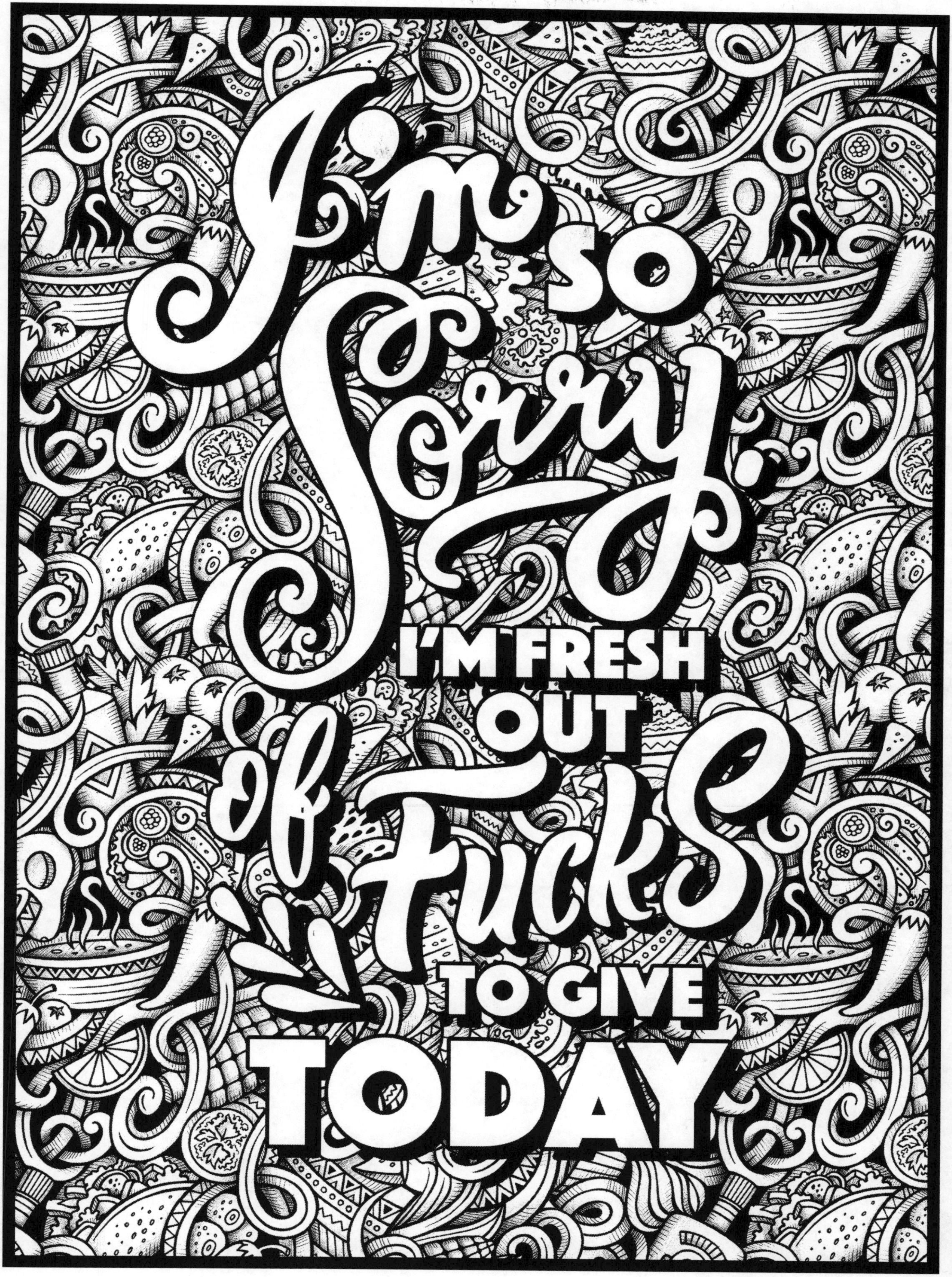
I'm so
Sorry.
I'M FRESH
OUT
of Fucks
TO GIVE
TODAY

Calm
UR
Tits

AIN'T NOBODY
GOT FUCKING TIME
for
that

I teach
THEREFORE
I drink

Want free goodies?
Email us at freebies@honeybadgercoloring.com

@honeybadgercoloring

Honey Badger Coloring

Shop our other books at
www.honeybadgercoloring.com

Wholesale distribution through Ingram Content Group
www.ingramcontent.com/publishers/distribution/wholesale

For questions and customer service, email us at
support@honeybadgercoloring.com

Made in the USA
Las Vegas, NV
25 November 2022

60296626R00059